Let's Start! ICT

Making Charts

Anne Rooney

QED Publishing

First published in the UK in 2005 by
QED Publishing
A Quarto Group company
226 City Road
London EC1V 2TT

www.qed-publishing.co.uk

A Catalogue record for this book is available from
the British Library.

ISBN 1 84538 191 2

Written by Anne Rooney
Consultant: Philip Stubbs
Editor: Louisa Somerville
Designer: Jacqueline Palmer
Illustrator: John Haslam
Photographer: Ray Moller
Models provided by Scallywags

Publisher: Steve Evans
Creative Director: Louise Morley
Editorial Manager: Jean Coppendale

Printed and bound in China

Words in bold **like this** are explained in the Glossary on page 30.

Contents

About Making Charts

You can often find out as much from pictures as from reading words. Some **information** is easier to understand in a picture.

Some facts can be shown clearly in a picture or chart.

Imagine you've looked into a rock pool on the beach. You might have found these sea creatures:

You might start by putting them in groups. This helps you to see more clearly what you've found.

This is called **sorting** or **classifying** objects.

Then you could count each group and make a chart like this one.

The chart is divided into bars, or columns. The size of the columns shows how many things you found.

Which is the tallest column? This shows that you found mostly shellfish.

This book shows you how to make and understand charts like this. They are called **pictograms**.

Finding out

To make your own pictogram you'll need to find out some information. There are lots of ways to do this. You can ask people, or count things or measure them.

What's your favourite ice-cream?

Information from other people

Sometimes you will get your information from other people. You could ask them questions or ask them to **vote** for a favourite of some kind.

Information from things

Lots of information comes from counting things.

You might count how many people in your class have dark hair, how many have fair hair and how many have red hair.

Colour of hair in our class

Brown hair ///////
Red hair //
Fair hair /////
Black hair ///

Weather at lunchtime

Monday = sunny

Tuesday = rainy

Wednesday = sunny

Thursday = cloudy

Friday = cloudy

You could record the weather at lunchtime for a week and list the days it rained, the days it was cloudy and the days it was sunny.

Asking questions

When you make a chart, you might get your information from other people.

You could ask people to put their hand up if a dog is their favourite pet, or a cat, and so on. You would need to count the hands each time.

Making a survey

You could do a **survey** instead. This is useful if the people you want to ask aren't in the same place at the same time. You write down your questions and ask people one at a time to give their answers.

Work out the best way to ask your question.

If you just ask people which animal is the scariest, you might get too many different answers to make a pictogram.

Which animal are you most scared of?

tiger /// crab,
tiger, lion,
scorpion, bee //
hippo
shark fierce dog wolf
snake shark //
wasp
slug

X

It's best to give people some answers to choose from. Then you know all the answers will fit your pictogram.

Which of these is the scariest animal?

shark ////
tiger //
lion ///
spider ////
wasp /

✓

sharks

Investigate

Another way to **investigate** is to do an experiment and **record** the results, or take measurements.

Fruit
apples ///////
bananas //
grapes /////
pears ///
oranges //

You could look at the type of fruit in everyone's lunchbox and write down which fruit people have brought to school.

Less is more!

Don't try to get too much information. A small number of choices is easier to record.

If you take measurements, make sure you always measure things in the same way so that you make a fair comparison.

When you record a measurement, use the nearest whole number.

bean 1

bean 2

height of beans
week 6

bean 1 = 5 cm

bean 2 = 4 cm

Enough!

Small numbers of things will make your chart easier for others to read.

Check it!

It's a good idea to check that you are getting your information in the best way. Some ways are better than others!

At the gate

Suppose you wanted to find out how children come to school. One way is to stand at the gate counting people as they arrive.

How children get to school

car //////////////////////
bus ////////////
on bike ////////////////////
on foot //////////////////

The hard way

It's hard to count the number of children in cars and buses, because lots of children may arrive at the same time.

A better way

It's better to go around the classes and ask how many people come to school by each type of transport.

class 2
30 children
car —/////////
bus —//////////
on bike —/////
on foot —/////

Final check

- Count the number of people in the survey and the number of ticks. Are they the same?
- Did you measure or count the right things?
- Did you ask the right questions?

Lines and piles

A pictogram shows a picture of each thing in a column or bar. It's not the same as making a line or a pile in real life.

Make a line

Ask everyone to bring their coats in from the cloakroom. Sort the coats by colour and put them in separate lines – red coats, blue ones and so on.

Count how many coats there are in each line. Some coats are bigger than others, so the most common coat colour may not make the longest line.

Pile them up

Now make piles of coats. Put each line of coloured coats into a separate pile.

Your piles are not like a pictogram. You can't tell from the height of the piles which is the most common colour.

Some coats may not fit your piles easily. You might need to start a new pile.

Neat and tidy

A pictogram would use the same size of picture for each coat. You could tell how many there are of each colour from the heights of the bars.

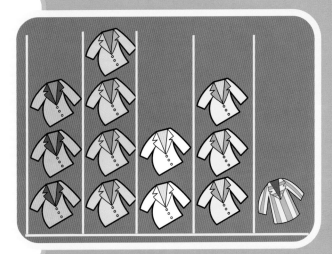

Looking good

To help people understand your chart it should be easy to read, and the pictures you use must suit your information.

Using icons

Your teacher will help you pick pictures that show what your chart is about. Pictures used like this are called **icons**.

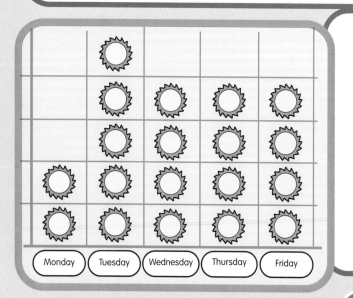

| Monday | Tuesday | Wednesday | Thursday | Friday |

You might use the same icon in each bar. If you had counted the hours of sunshine each day for a week, you might put suns in each bar.

The icons might be completely different. If your chart shows the fruit people have in their lunchboxes, you might use a different fruit picture in each bar.

How many icons?

Look at the information you have gathered for your chart. Does it need just one icon or lots of different icons? If it needs lots, which ones?

Start a chart

It's time to practise putting information into a chart on the computer.

click cat column

then click cat four times to enter 4 cats

Getting started

You may be able to choose how many columns to have on your pictogram.

You may be able to give a name, or label, to each column.

Type the numbers or click a button for each number. If you wanted to enter '4' for the cats column, click on the cat picture four times.

Get it right!

If you make a mistake, put it right. When you've finished, check the numbers again by looking at the information you found out.

Pets in our class

dogs 2

cats 4

rabbits 3

fish 4

birds 1

- Have you copied all the numbers correctly?

- Have you missed any numbers out?

Making sense

You know what the chart is about – but other people need to be able to read it, too.

Year 1 lunchboxes

How we get to school

How many in my family

Favourite fish

Use a title

You'll need a title that explains what the chart shows. Make it short but clear.

Numbers

Putting numbers up the side of the chart helps people see how many things there are in each column without having to count them.

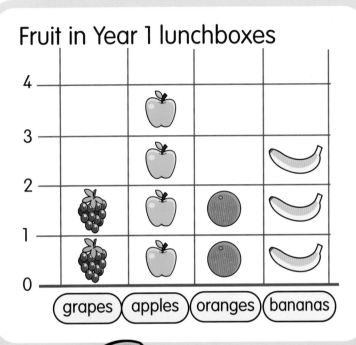

Fruit in Year 1 lunchboxes

grapes apples oranges bananas

Anything else?

You can put the date on your chart if it will help people to understand it. If it is a weather chart, it matters whether it was in summer or winter. Four sunny days in a row would be more surprising in the winter than in the summer!

What does it mean?

Looking at a pictogram can tell you a lot of information.

How many?

You can see from the height of each bar how many things are in each group.

You can see how many children have each colour in their bedroom. How many people have pink bedrooms?

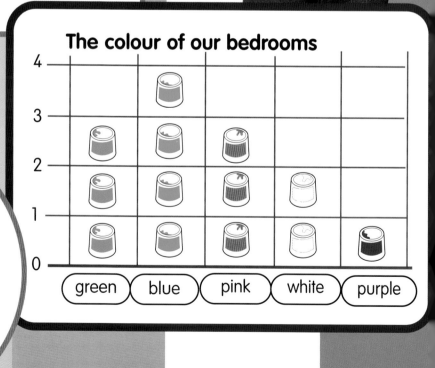

The colour of our bedrooms

4
3
2
1
0

green   blue   pink   white   purple

Picking favourites

Compare the size of the bars. The tallest bar shows you which is the most common colour.

The most common colour of bedroom is blue. Pink and green are the second most common colours.

The least common colour is purple – only one person has a purple bedroom.

Comparing

The bar for blue bedrooms is twice as tall as the bar for white bedrooms. This tells you that twice as many people have blue bedrooms as white bedrooms.

What doesn't it mean?

It's good to know what a chart shows you – but it's important to remember there are some things it doesn't show you.

Take care!

In the chart, more people have blue bedrooms than any other colour – but that doesn't mean most people have blue bedrooms.

Of the 13 bedrooms in the chart only four are blue – that's less than half!

You can't say that blue is the children's favourite colour for bedrooms.

They might not have been allowed to choose the colour. Or they might share a bedroom with a brother or sister and had to agree on a colour they both quite like.

You can't tell...

You can't tell from the chart which child has which colour.

You can't tell whether more girls than boys have pink bedrooms.

You can't tell whether older children all have blue bedrooms.

You can't tell if shared bedrooms are more likely to be painted white.

Over to you

Now it's time to make a pictogram of your own.

Which sport do you like best?

What pets do you have?

Choosing a subject

Decide what your pictogram will show. Here are some ideas, but you could choose something totally different:

- What sorts of pets people have.

- Favourite sports.

- Types of trees – in your garden, at school or in the park.

Getting information

Work out exactly what information you need. Remember to ask your question in the same way every time. Make sure people understand the question and the type of answer you need.

Don't choose a subject that will be too difficult to investigate.

- If you are counting things or people, make sure your numbers are right.

- If you look at how people come to school, are you going to count people or types of transport?

- If you look at fruit in lunchboxes, don't count each grape separately!

Making your chart

Put your information into the computer. Check that you've put it in properly and correct any mistakes. Choose icons that show what your pictogram is about, and add labels.

Favourite sports

	football	netball	swimming	tennis	riding

What have you found out?

What can you tell from your chart? Which is the top sport? Do children prefer apples or oranges for lunch?

What don't you know?

What sort of information can't you tell from your chart? Is the information you've got the most useful? Or might people want to know different facts?

Check your work

Think about how you've made your chart.

- Would different icons have been better?

- Could you have used clearer labels?

- Did you ask enough people?

- Can you make the chart any better?

Glossary

Classify   Put objects into groups.

Icon   Small picture that stands for something.

Information   Facts about something.

Investigate   Find out about something.

Pictogram   Chart that shows how many things there are of different sorts by showing pictures in a column, or bar.

Record   Write down information.

Sort   Put objects into groups.

Survey   Ask people questions and write down their answers.

Vote   Show which you prefer or choose a favourite.

Index

Grown-up zone

Making Charts
and the National Curriculum

The work in this book will help children to cover the following parts of the National Curriculum ICT scheme of work: unit 1e, part of unit 1c. It can be tied in with work on science and maths.

Make sure the pictogram software is set up ready for the children to use. They will need suitable icons to be available. You will need to choose suitable text fonts and sizes.

Encourage children to work together and discuss options as they collect information and make their pictograms. Ask them to state what they are trying to find out. This will make it possible to assess how successful they were. Review their finished work and ask them to talk about why they chose the options they did, and why they rejected others. Ask them if they can think of any ways of improving their work.

Children should be encouraged to review, evaluate and improve their own work at all stages. If possible, show them work by older children and help them to see how this fulfils the same aims that they have in their own work.